FROM

Hatred

TO

Healing
Eight Racial Reconciliation Poems

Alicea Davis

Esteem Builders Publications Co.
Pontiac, MI USA

"Publishing books that heal, empower
and build up the minds of others
for the betterment of society."

From Hatred to Healing: Eight Racial Reconciliation Poems
© 2016 Alicea Davis.

All rights reserved worldwide. No part of this publication may be reproduced, stored in a retrieval system, or transmitted in any form or by any means – electronic, mechanical, photocopy, recording, or any other – except for brief quotations in printed reviews, without the prior permission of the publisher.

All Scriptures taken from the Holy Bible, New International Version®, NIV®. Copyright © 1973, 1978, 1984, 2011 by Biblica, Inc.™ Used by permission of Zondervan. All rights reserved worldwide. www.zondervan.com The "NIV" and "New International Version" are trademarks registered in the United States Patent and Trademark Office by Biblica, Inc.™

Published by
Esteem Builders Publications Co.
Pontiac, MI 48343 USA
info@EsteemBuildersPublications.com
www.EsteemBuildersPublications.com

For more information, contact
www.AliceaDavis.com

ISBN 13:   978-0-997671-0-4   Paperback

Editing by Patricia Hicks
Cover and interior design by Christina Dixon

Printed in the United States of America

DEDICATION

This book is dedicated to my husband, Benjamin. Your love and support is incomparable. And to my family, who patiently prayed for me until I found my healing.

TABLE OF CONTENTS

Dedication .... *i*

Introduction .... *v*

Heal My Hatred 1

Grateful * 5

A Secret to Success * 9

Unite and Conquer * 13

True Re**search** 17

I Reconcile with Me 21

Above Revenge 25

God is Healing 29

About the Author 31

* Indicates poems previously published in author's first work entitled, *The Sky is NOT the Limit: A Book of Empowering Poetry.*

INTRODUCTION

This book of poetry begins near the end of the dark tunnel of my suffering from hatred within. Thankfully, relief will soon arrive in these pages, as the weight of hatred is lifted and minds become adjusted to the light. Throughout this poetic journey we will focus more on healing, allowing hope to spring forth. The words, *From Hatred to Healing*, is more than just my book title, it is also my prayer for my country – America.

I know first-hand and from the many testimonials I've received, that the messages in these poems can heal others overwhelmed by racial injustice – on both sides of the divide. I hope this book will continue to inspire individuals to be among the first in their circles of influence to open their arms and embrace more unity in America.

As for me, living the rest of my life filled with anger and hate was not an option. So, I prayed for God to set me free through my gift of poetry. Today I am walking in my healing. I have compiled these poems to help others move forward toward the light of racial reconciliation.

 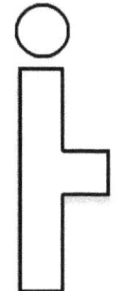

HEAL MY HATRED

Lord,

This anger and hate is a weight that is too great.

These headlines of death now have me predicting my fate.

But I am tired because I am changing for the worse.

A bitter past and a bloody future is all that my mind will rehearse.

So, I need Your help to put this hatred in reverse.

My light is supposed to shine in this dark world that I am in.

I know that as your child, this hatred is a sin.

My soul is in a battle, and I want to win.

But the racism and murders are affecting me, and I cannot play pretend.

I need a change that is real.

This pain needs to heal.

Because centuries of oppression have time standing still.

Yet my heart still longs to be in Your will.

Your Word says for me not to lean on my own understanding,

and that You will give me peace beyond my understanding.

Well help me, Lord, because what I understand

is that people of color may not be safe in this land.

Will You give us a hand?

This anger has turned my whole world upside down.

What used to be a constant smile is now a steady frown.

I have been poisoned with fear, and that makes me mad.

Which led to the hate, and now I feel bad.

I just want back the light that I have always had.

I need a spiritual deliverance from the anger and hate.

Otherwise, I am dead already, but my funeral will have to wait.

I can be a zombie until the day You call me home.

Because I am just the living dead, if all of my hope is gone.

Or I can trust that since You specialize in resurrection,

You can get my country headed in the right direction.

But let the change begin in me.

From anger and hatred, I want to be set free.

So that I can be the light that You created me to be.

I am casting my cares on Thee,

because a positive change is something that I want to see.

 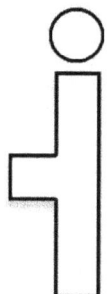

GRATEFUL

This message is for all of the whites.

who've always had the desire to love and unite.

You were the ones who had our backs

and did not prejudge us because we are black.

You are more than an exception

To all the hatred and rejection.

You were our trusted ally,

when we needed help to get by.

You were against all the suffering that we went through.

As we wept at night, you cried too.

And we are so grateful,

for you not being hateful.

In a time when discrimination is still tried and true,

we have to give credit to whom honor is due.

Today, when I needed a job to pay my bills

you didn't focus on my color, but you respected my skills.

Yesterday, when we marched, I know you took pride.

As we protested for civil rights, you were right by our side.

And the day before, when the slaves hid underground,

my family took shelter in your home,

But you pretended that they were not around.

And we are so grateful

for you not being hateful.

Especially during the times

when loving us was a crime.

You risked your own kindred's respect and trust

all in the name of helping us.

You celebrated Emancipation, you were dancing and drinking,

instead of questioning, "What was Lincoln thinking?"

It is amazing through all the pain and insanity

how you managed to keep your love and humanity.

You let your children play with us.

You came to church to pray with us.

It is nice to see you more than every once in a while,

still greeting us with your welcoming smile.

Even though we still have room to grow,

we appreciate you and we want you to know

that we still need you.

Because uniting humanity is what we can do.

I see you, my friend,

making it easier as our struggle comes closer to an end.

But the truth is,

there are still some inequalities out there,

but we know better than to think that you do not care.

That's why we are so grateful

for you not being hateful.

Thank you.

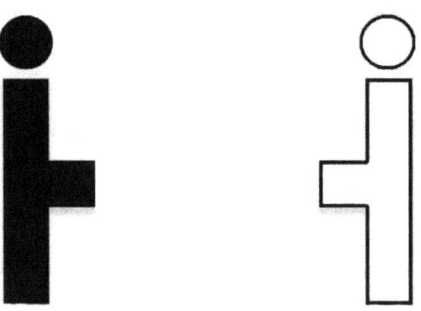

A SECRET TO SUCCESS

There is something that you owe yourself,

if you want good health and a life full of wealth.

Because God has some major plans for you,

but first, you have some inner work to do.

There is a reason why your dreams don't last.

It's because you have been holding on to your past.

It eats away at your success

this anger and pain that was repressed.

I know that person put trauma on you,

and acted as if there's just drama on you.

But only you are carrying this heavy load,

because they barely even remember that episode.

They may have tested you or rejected you,

and you want to hold a grudge like the rest would do.

But you must let go,

because you will not be able to grow.

It will be so many years wasted before you realize that you were emotionally paralyzed.

All those projects you started, that never got finished,

was because a piece of your soul was diminished.

But when you let go of your past, you will be replenished.

You must release the pain they put you through,

and break the chains that are binding you.

This same relief has happened to me.

and it feels so good to live so free!

Your true purpose in life will come and find you.

Once you have the courage to leave your past behind you.

It doesn't matter if the tears

have been flowing for many years.

Even strangers can identify who you are,

because of how soon you show them your scar.

You are in denial, but you think you are fine.

The truth is, you are living in past time.

Whether you were shot, abused, however disrespected,

what is done, is done, and only you can accept it.

It may be hard to believe, but after a while,

they may decide to reconcile.

But if they are still rejecting, you can't stop.

Because their jaws will drop

once you make it to the top.

But first it has to be in your heart to forgive.

Then a prosperous life you are sure to live.

And the fortune that I am talking about,

you will possess both inside and out.

And your bright future will prove the rest

if you apply to your life, this secret to success.

Forgive.

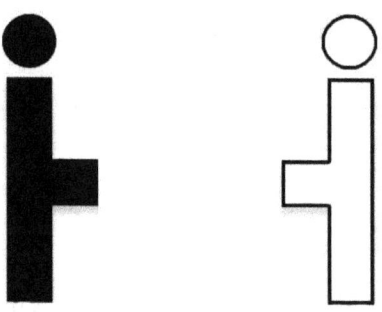

UNITE AND CONQUER

A nation that is divided will fall.

So we all must come together to build up a wall.

As long as there is division between white and black,

we're all more vulnerable to this country being attacked.

In the best interest of this land remaining free,

we have to invest in a bond between you and me.

But this division will never come to an end,

if we keep ignoring where our story begins.

Establishing unity requires your mental bravery,

realizing today's blacks and whites are both victims of slavery.

Whether you come from an owner or from a slave,

we're all walking on a road that we didn't even pave.

We have to accept this mind-boggling reality,

that even some whites are mental victims of slavery's brutality.

You may have certain views and opinions as a white,

that makes you uncomfortable and they don't feel right.

You try to go back in your mind to the first day,

you started perceiving the black community in a negative way.

To discover the entire truth, you will have to rewind

your mind back to slavery times.

Freeing the slaves may have affected the country's bottom line,

but changing the laws will not change a person's mind.

The past has possibly made you a victim too.

Society has embedded these hurtful views into you.

It's no wonder you think the way that you do.

Living your life as if the stereotypes are true.

The slave owner's mentality, your heart must fight it

so all the citizens in this country can be united.

The fact that this country is now diverse

Must be accepted and not be reversed.

We all have dominion over the earth's food chain.

Why cause a fellow human being hurt and pain?

When you explore other galaxies in outer space,

you'll find that we earthlings can only survive in this place.

Why judge another because of their race,

if you love the color that is on your face?

It is unity that will keep this country strong.

So we all must feel like we belong.

This is not a one-sided quest for unity.

I must also build up the mindsets in my own community.

I am challenging us all to face and conquer our past.

Is that too much for me to ask?

TRUE RE**SEARCH**

The media

cannot replace the encyclopedia.

Because the evening news

profits from your fears and blues.

If you were to perceive black lives

with a fresh pair of eyes,

you might be surprised,

that the majority of us don't have mug shots.

We are making the most of what we've got.

If your social media friends have the same mindset that you do,

then you may be reaffirming misconceptions that are not true.

How will you grow

if you're only exposed to the viewpoints you already know?

Doing some true research will help you to see

that I am not who the media portrays me to be.

Visit our churches, universities and prosperous neighborhoods.

You'll see our hope despite our history of being misunderstood.

Doing some true research will help you to see

what you've been missing when you look at me.

I RECONCILE WITH ME

African.

Slave.

Negro.

Colored.

Black.

African-American.

My people and I have been processing our identity for centuries.

But today, I am accepting who I am. I mean all of me.

Even the part of me I can no longer deny.

I'm accepting a truth that can make so many of us cry.

I'm embracing the fact that the blood in my veins is not 100% African pure.

The shade of my skin makes me absolutely sure,

that although there are no chains on my body or in my mind,

my ancestor's slave master is still easy to find.

Where does he exist today?
He can be discovered in my DNA.
You see, he violated my great-great-great grandmother one night,
and she would have been killed if she put up a fight.
Nine months later, she gave birth,
to a beautiful culture that contributes much to this earth.
I'm talking about my people, as we continue to discover our worth.
Yet I am more than a product of slavery.
I am more than a reminder of my ancestor's bravery.
I am a soul that is totally free
because I even accept the slave master in me.
When faced with this truth, I had a decision to make.
To press on towards the future or live in self-hate.
The courage to accept my truth was heaven sent.
Making me potent.
The power has been invested in me
to both extend and accept his apology.

I reconcile with me!

Because I am the only one that I can control.

So I unite the opposition in my soul.

Making two once fragmented pieces a unique whole.

Accepting what my heart wanted to reject

has brought forth wholeness and self-respect.

I can contribute to society with the mindset to delegate,

but with a heart to do it without the hate.

I'm a visionary with a soul that's willing to get down into the trenches.

I see God bridging the racial divide by the miles and by the inches.

That's why I believe in an America that's free at last,

free from chains and guilt from the present and the past.

I know that the future I see

is more than a possibility,

because I am able to reconcile with me.

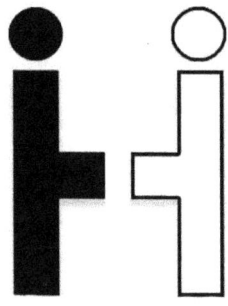

ABOVE REVENGE

I do not wish to see you in chains.

Oppressing you for 400 years will not validate the pain.

There is no such thing as revenge for this catastrophe and loss,

because it would be impossible to calculate the cost.

If I were to give you 100 lashes, what difference would it make?

Would breaking up your family show you that you made a huge mistake?

That would not cause my ancestors to resurrect.

That would not teach black children self-respect.

The hope that I have which is truly near me,

is for you to realize that you never had a reason to fear me.

Because I am not low,

revenge is beneath me and you should know,

that I fly high and I want to let the record show,

that I am healed.

So to hatred and un-forgiveness I will not yield.

Because underneath my beautiful skin is a soul that belongs to God,

with the mind of Jesus Christ, though to some it may be odd,

how I am not ashamed to say,

that His blood also washed your sins away.

I only look forward to the day

When the irrational fears will fade away.

I am not low.

revenge is beneath me and you should know,

that I fly high and I want to let the record show,

I refuse to become your foe.

Slavery being wrong is a point that has already been proved.

God's healing power has caused my pain to be removed.

There is no reason to go back and forth.

We all have value. We all have worth.

I just want to move on with my life,

in a country that is free from oppression and strife.

Today, I am too busy enjoying opportunities and infinite possibilities.

So seeking revenge on you will hinder my stabilities.

This is a chance for you to heal and grow,

By simply realizing that I am not low.

Revenge is beneath me and you should know,

that I fly high and I want to let the record show,

I am a vessel overflowing with God's love,

Making revenge a matter that I am above.

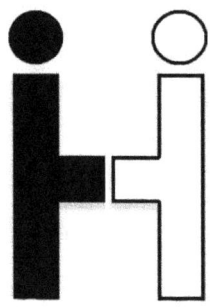

GOD IS HEALING

God is healing the world with one country at a time.

He is healing the countries with one community at a time.

He is healing the communities with one family at a time.

He is healing the families with one relationship at a time.

He is healing the relationships with one person at a time.

And He is using me to heal the people

With just one poem at a time.

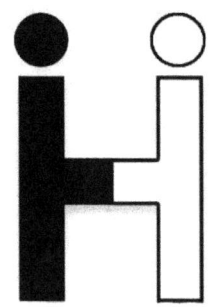

ABOUT THE AUTHOR

God is healing and empowering the minds of others through the uplifting poetry and insightful artwork of Alicea Davis. She has been writing poetry for over 25 years which began in her childhood. She is passionate about creating work that will be a resource of light in our world.

Born and raised in Detroit, MI, Alicea launches projects that the whole world can experience. Her first book entitled; *The Sky is NOT the Limit: A Book of Empowering Poetry,* inspires readers to transition from the darkness of fear, into the light of trust in multiple areas of life. *From Hatred to Healing: Eight Racial Reconciliation Poems* is her second book of poetry.

Davis is also a talented visual artist. Her paintings communicate deep truths and emotions that words alone cannot convey. Davis has shared her messages with the masses on television, radio, at universities and more. Visit her website www.AliceaDavis.com to learn more about her and her work.

The following quotes encouraged me as I prepared to reach others with the messages in this book.

I share them with you in hopes that these words of wisdom will also inspire more racial reconciliation today.

- Alicea Davis

"We in this country, in this generation, are by – destiny rather than choice – the watchmen on the walls of world freedom. We ask, therefore, that we may be worthy of our power and responsibility, that we may exercise our strength with wisdom and restraint, and that we may achieve in our time and for all time the ancient vision of 'peace on earth, and good will toward men.' That must always be our goal, and the righteousness of our cause must always underlie our strength. For as was written long ago: 'except the Lord keep the city, the watchman waketh but in vain.'"

- President John F. Kennedy

The final paragraph of the speech President John F. Kennedy was to deliver in Dallas on November 22, 1963.

Kennedy, John F.: John F. Kennedy Presidential Library and Museum [https://www.jfklibrary.org/Research/Research-Aids/JFK-Speeches/Dallas-TX-Trade-Mart-Undelivered_19631122.aspx] [August 26, 2016]

"All this is from God, who reconciled us to himself through Christ and gave us the ministry of reconciliation."

- The Apostle Paul

The Holy Bible: 2 Corinthians 5:18

"Love your neighbor as yourself."
- Jesus Christ
My Lord and Savior

The Holy Bible: Matthew 22:39b

**"Do to others
as you would have them do to you."**

- Jesus Christ
My Lord and Savior

The Holy Bible: Luke 6:31

www.ingramcontent.com/pod-product-compliance
Lightning Source LLC
Chambersburg PA
CBHW070553300426
44113CB00011B/1897